NAS guide

Network Attached Storage (NAS, English for network-connected storage).

With this guide, I would like to help a little bit so that you can easily assemble a simple and inexpensive NAS yourself.

For the Open Media Vault operating system, which I use here, there are countless other options that can be used.

I limit myself to the main usage of a NAS and that is to provide storage over the network.

This is a NAS with web server for backup and data backup.

Have fun setting up and building yourself.

Table of Content

Hardware and Software

Hardware

The following hardware can be used. In detail, you have to check again yourself whether it really should be the hardware.

Raspberry 4 package

USB HDD

Monitor with HDMI

USB keyboard

Disused computers and laptops can also be used as such. Or you can build a completely new PC.

Software

The following free tools are required for some steps.

Open Media Vault (NAS operating system)

https://www.openmediavault.org/

WinSCP (data copying tool)

https://winscp.net/eng/index.php

Putty (command line)

https://www.putty.org/

Advanced IP Scanner (network scan)

https://www.advanced-ip-scanner.com/de/

Allways Sync (automatically synchronize data)

https://allwaysync.com/download/?lang=de-at

Win32DiskImager (write images to removable disk)

https://sourceforge.net/projects/win32diskimager/

Installation

Install via SD card

For the Raspberry, there is a really easy way to install it. The Win32DiskImage tool is installed for this.

The current OMV downloaded as an image. Insert the SD card into the PC.

1. Select image

2. Select removable media

3. Write to write the image

As soon as the process is successfully completed. Remove the SD card from the PC and insert it into the Raspberry. Now connect to the Raspberry USB keyboard, monitor, network and power. The keyboard and monitor are no longer needed later. In theory, this is not used at the beginning.

With some OMV versions the "SSH" must be activated. "SSH" is the command line connection to the NAS. We can easily start this later via the webgui if it is needed.

If a monitor and keyboard are connected, you should now be able to log in.

If you have nothing further, then the IP must first be found.

Find the IP of the OMV

Our OMV NAS is ready for operation (power plugged in, switched on) and connected to the router with a network cable.

In Windows, click on Start. Then enter "cmd" in the program search.

Select "cmd.exe" from the list above.

Now a command line opens.

Enter the command "ipconfig" and enter.

The following issue should appear.

Where the arrow is, that is the IP of your own PC.

Now we can search our network with the "Advanced IP Scanner" tool.

You have to download this tool beforehand and either install it or simply run it.

At 1. Now enter the IP range. In this case 192.168.0.1 - 192.168.0.254. Now scan the network. And lo and behold, our NAS has been found. We have given the name "testnas" here. I was able to give the name because I used an ISO file and installed it on a PC.

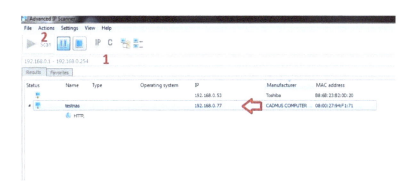

First Login

With this IP, we can log into the OMV Webgui in the browser of our choice.

At the top of the address line, enter the IP address and Enter. Now the webgui should open with a login.

Webgui is a user interface and looks like a normal website from the Internet. (as a little explanation)

Standard accounts

WebGUI

User: admin

Password: openmediavault

Client (SSH, console)

User: root

Password: openmediavault

Activate SSH

After registering, we first activate the SSH

In the left riding we look for the SSH and click on it.

Now there is a new window, activate it as follows and save everything.

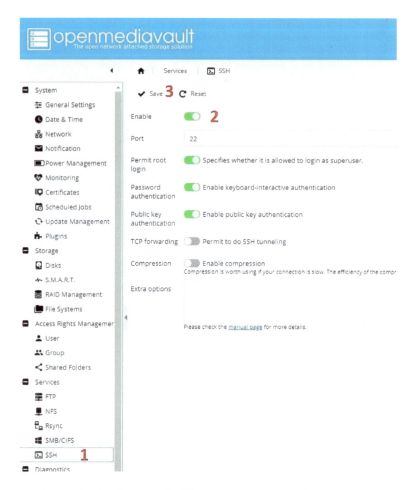

In the end, the OMV asks if you want to use it.

1. Must then be applied after every configuration change.

Create user

1. User in the left bar

2. adding

3. Give your name

4. Email address

5. Assign password

6. Repeat password

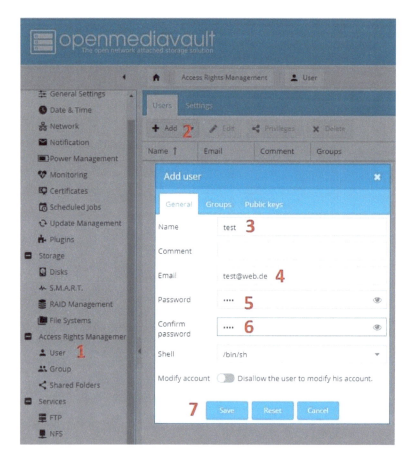

Now select the groups. Our user should be assigned to the following groups.

Sambashare and SSH is important to have access to the data release afterwards. Therefore, at least these should be selected, if you intend to use this user. And save and apply everything again.

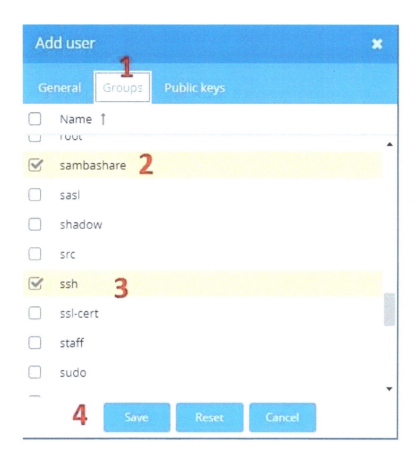

Set up RAID

If you have several hard disks, they can be combined to form a network. A RAID 1 makes sense here. Here two hard disks become one. Now it is the case that the two hard drives are mirrored together. The advantage is that if one of the hard drives should fail, then all data will remain without loss. Disadvantage, you only have the capacity of a hard disk.

1. RAID management

2. Create

3. Assign the name of the drive

4th level assigned, Mirror is our RAID 1 and reflects the data

5. Select hard drives

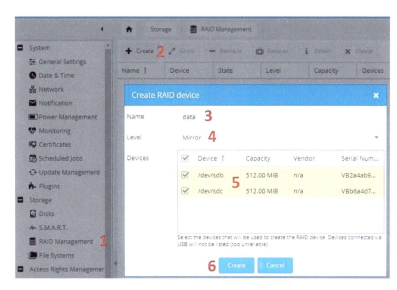

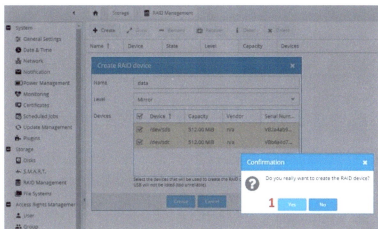

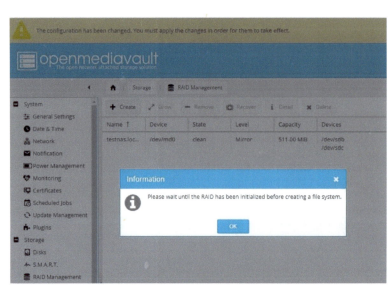

Set up file system

After creating our RAID or just connecting a hard drive, we need to create the file system so that the hard drive can be used for data.

4. Assign a name for the HDD e.g. Data

5. Choose file system e.g. EXT4 (it depends a little on what you have to do with the NAS, you would then have to read the individual file systems to find out what their advantages are) EXT4 is quite robust, so it is safer but also slower, but you don't notice anything like that.

All other points are self-explanatory.

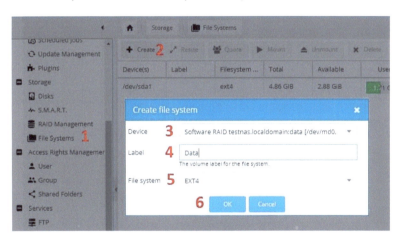

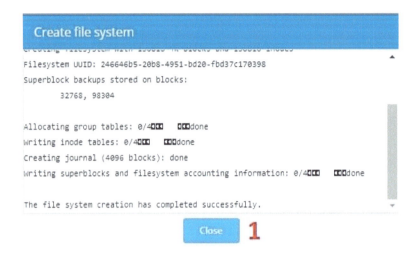

After the file system has been created, the drive must now be mounted. It is now known to OMV and can be used.

And apply and save everything.

Email dispatch

If you want to receive regular signs of life or other important information such as hard disk problems as email, you should set up email sending.

1. Notification

2. Activate

3. Enter the SMTP server of the email server. At Web.de this should be found in Settings.

4. Enter the port

5. Activate secure connection, web host should allow this

6. Email address

7. Activate to use a registration

8. How to log in to Web.de or the other host

9. password

10. Where to send what

11. save

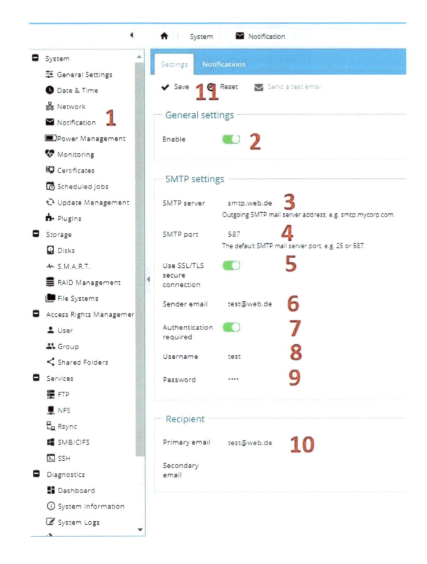

Smart monitoring

Now it also makes sense to set up smart monitoring. Smart monitoring detects small errors on hard drives. If the first errors occur, the hard drive should be replaced quickly to prevent the hard drive from failing completely. This means that hard drive errors are detected earlier and total losses prevented. Unfortunately, however, it cannot provide complete protection, as hard disks can break even without extensive notice.

Now we set it up. The first thing to do is to activate SMART.

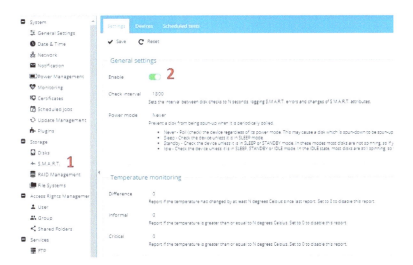

Now activate for the individual hard drives. In our example, 3 hard drives are installed, where it can be activated.

Set up file sharing

Now we want to use the NAS for what it actually is. Namely, be a data store over the network.

1. Add shared folder

2. adding

3. Name for the folder

4. Select hard disk

5. The path

6. Access rights. Here you have more choice. It is possible to block all others except the admin access.

7. Don't forget to save

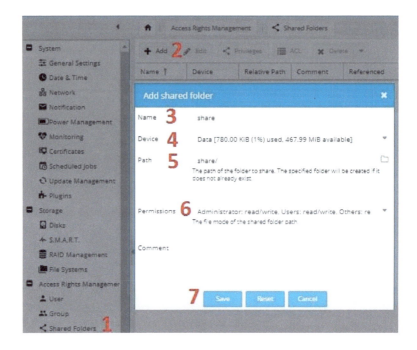

Here at the release I want that only our test user has access and is also the owner of this release. This is done as follows.

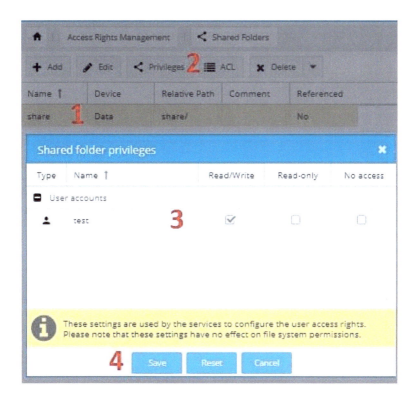

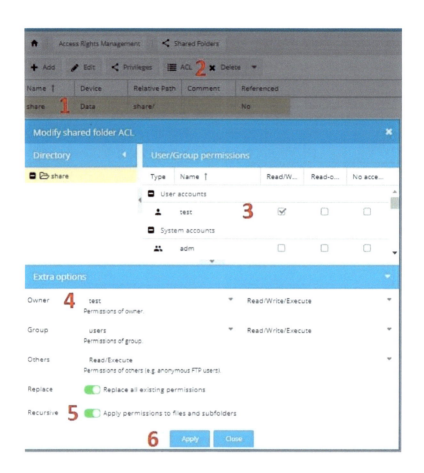

Set up Samba sharing

Samba is the release to make the NAS storage available to the Windows PC.

Here are the individual steps. Our "testshare" should now be selectable under shared folders.

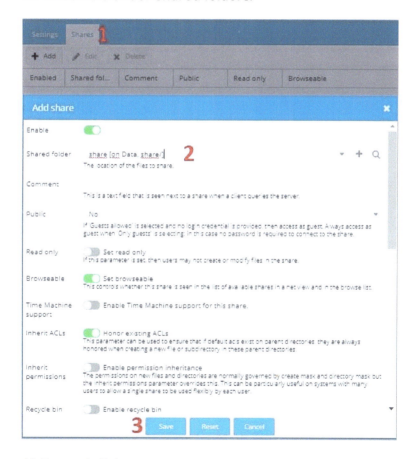

At the end click on save.

Now activate the Samba service under Settings.

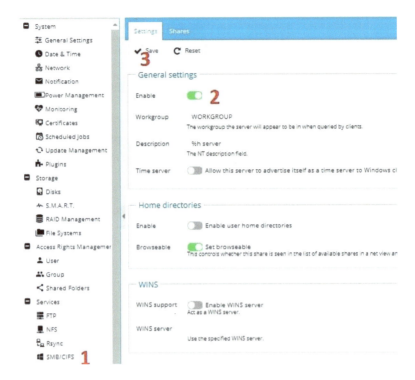

At the end save and activate everything again.

Now enter the following under Windows, Start in the program search. \\ 192.168.0.77

Now a window should open for registration.

There, enter the respective user that you had previously created. In our case.

User: test

Password: test

Our release should now be visible. Now click on it with the right mouse button. The following appears.

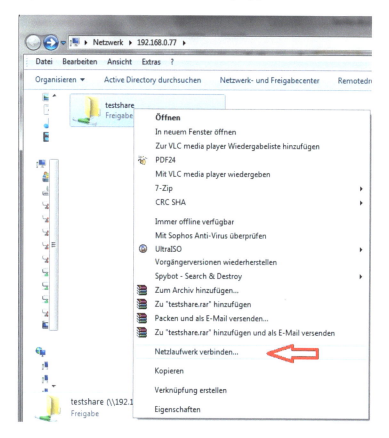

Network Connect at the arrow.

Connect to network drive there. Now another window opens. There is no need to make any further settings there. Therefore simply click on "Finish".

Now open "Computer". Then our Windows partition should be visible there and our "testshare"

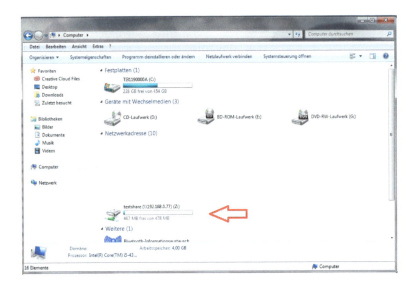

Now the data can be saved on it as if it were an internal hard drive.

The hard disk should reappear there every time you boot.

If you do not want to log in with a password every time, to access the data. Then simply tick the box next time you log in and save your login details.

Easy backup of the Windows folder

Now you want to synchronize a folder that you have on the internal hard drive with the NAS hard drive. Then the tool "Allway Sync" helps.

You can download it here for free.

https://allwaysync.com

Now after it has been installed. Add a new job.

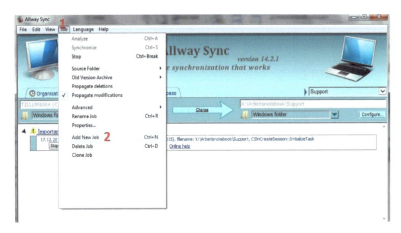

Now give the new project a name. To do this, right-click and rename on the "New Project" tab.

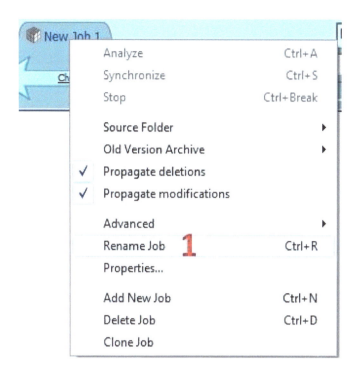

Now a folder must be specified on the left and right. To do this, click the "Search" button and select the respective folder. At 1. "change", there the directions and the deletion behavior can be set up. I have set it up so that it is deleted and copied in both directions. Has the advantage, no matter in which folder you make a change, they are always the same.

Now the button at 2.Synchronieren and then it should look something like this.

Since it should happen completely automatically, you still have to set this up.

To do this, right-click on the "test" project. Click on Properties. A new window is opening up.

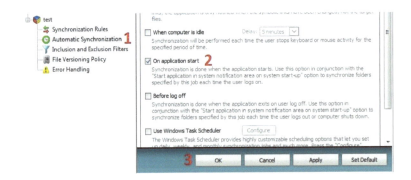

There at "Automatic synchronization". Then put the check mark at "At program start" and now on "Apply" and "ok".

Now when the Windows computer starts up, the program should start automatically and synchronize immediately in the background.

On Windows. "Start", "All Programs" in "Autostart". The entry "Allway Sync" should appear there.

Remote access via the Internet

If you want to access your data with the computer outside of your own network (for example via the Internet), it becomes a little more difficult.

As background knowledge. The Internet IP often changes daily. That is why there are services like DynDNS that convert this IP into a fixed name and that you can use it for access. To do this, look in its router to see which provider it allows. My routers are only paid services. Since I don't need the service all the time, I decided to use a free version. Although this is a little more complex, it is completely sufficient for me.

First of all, we need to know which Internet IP our router assigns.

You can see this at https://www.wieistmeineip.de/.

However, since we are not at home every day to check this out, we enter a task in our OMV NAS that allows us to receive the IP by email every day.

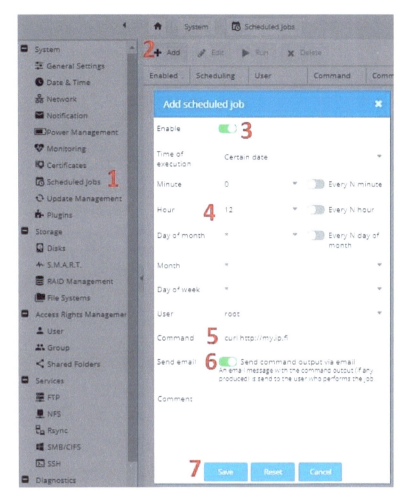

The important command is "curl http://my.ip.fi"

My router always restarts at night, so the test at 8 a.m.

The email should look something like this.

% Total % Received % Xferd Average Speed Time Time Time Current
Dload Upload Total Spent Left Speed

0 0 0 0 0 0 0 0 --:--:-- --:--:-- --:--:-- 0
100 13 100 13 0 0 56 0 --:--:-- --:--:-- --:--:-- 56
77.13.33.181

At the end is the IP address.

Now we have to set up our router. A port forwarding must be set up there. As soon as a request comes from there via the port, it should be sent to our NAS.

For this you have to enter the IP of the router in the browser. If you do not know this, then the Windows Commandline can help again. There the command "ipconfig" and the correct IP should be under Standard gateway.

After logging in to the router, look for the punk "Port Forwarding"

Enter a rule with port 22 and save the whole.

Data access with WinSCP over the Internet

Now get the "WinSCP" tool.
https://winscp.net/eng/index.php

After installation, a new connection must be set up under New Site.

Under the host name, the Internet IP. This must then be changed daily as soon as you want to access it again.
Enter the file protocol on SFP and the user and password.

Save everything and it should look like this.

Then also login. Another security question comes up. Confirm this with "yes" and after successful setup, you have access to your data. In the home network, the IP address of the NAS can also be used and the tool tested.

Restart automatically

Every now and then it is an advantage to restart the NAS. Because logs are full and the NAS just hangs. Other reasons are also possible. Therefore, it makes sense to have the NAS restart automatically after a certain time. It is not difficult. Simply add a "planned task" in the energy management. It's best to have it done once a week at night.

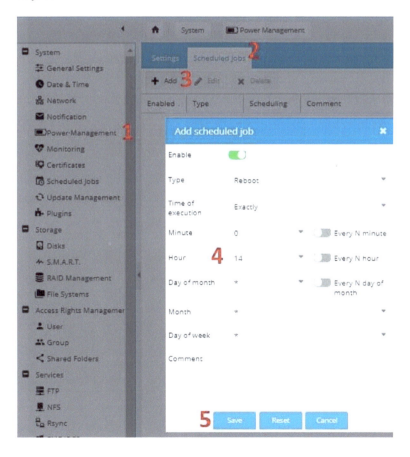

Update OMV

The OMV should also be updated from time to time. Here's how to do it.

1. Select "Update management" in the left bar

2. Now check for newer packages

3. Check mark for everyone

4. Perform update

Important is. It may happen that OMV no longer starts. Therefore, you should consider beforehand whether the data is needed right now. A backup should also be done. I also show how to do that.

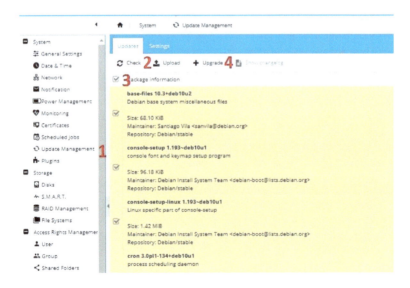

Log out or shutdown

Once all settings have been made, you can log out on the right-hand side. Shutting down is of course also possible.

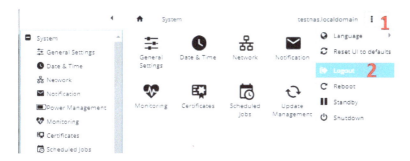

Save configuration and restore

Backup

An important point is to save the OMV configuration. Unfortunately, OMV has not yet had a direct function for this. In any case, the OVM can still be backed up by a small detour.

The Putty tool is required.

Enter the IP address of the OMV in the Hostname field.

And put on SSH.

Now click "open"

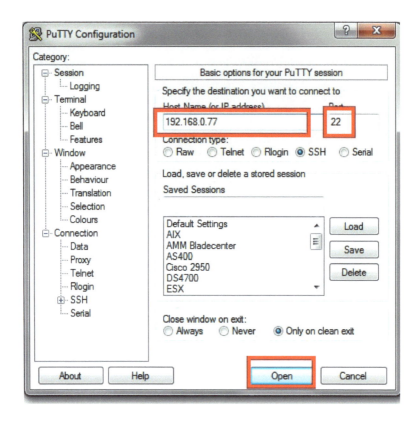

Now a security question comes up. Confirm this with "yes".

Log in with "root". So with "Login as: root" and enter. Then comes the query for the password.

Now the command. „df"

root@testnas:~# df

Output looks like this.

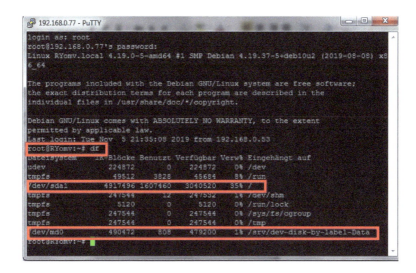

/dev/sda. Is in our case the boot hard disk.

/dev/md0 is the RAID 1. Here we need a folder where we want to save the backup. So you could find out.

Change to the folder with "cd" and "ls" to display the content.

root@testnas:~# cd /srv/dev-disk-by-label-Data

root@testnas:/srv/dev-disk-by-label-Data# ls

lost+found testshare

root@testnas:/srv/dev-disk-by-label-Data# cd testshare/

root@testnas:/srv/dev-disk-by-label-Data/testshare#

root@testnas:~# cd

This is Backup command.

```
root@testnas:~# sudo dd if=/dev/sda | gzip > /srv/dev-disk-by-label-Data/testshare/backup05112019.img.gz
```

Restore

```
root@testnas:~# gzip -cd /srv/dev-disk-by-label-Data/testshare/backup05112019.img.gz | sudo dd of=/dev/sda
```

2. NAS as a backup

If you have a 2nd NAS in use. Could you also use this to synchronize the data on another NAS.

I have two OMVs with one HDD each. This has the advantage whether an HDD or a complete system breaks down. A NAS should still be running and I can get my data. Whereby a NAS is always the boss and all access runs over it. The 2nd NAS only runs on the side and is at least not available via remote, but at any time within the network.

Set up server side

This is usually the backup server. So the one that runs alongside.

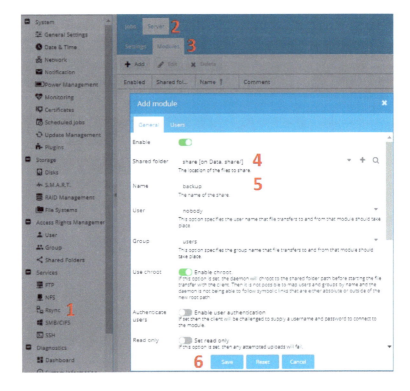

Which folder should now receive the data must be
selected.

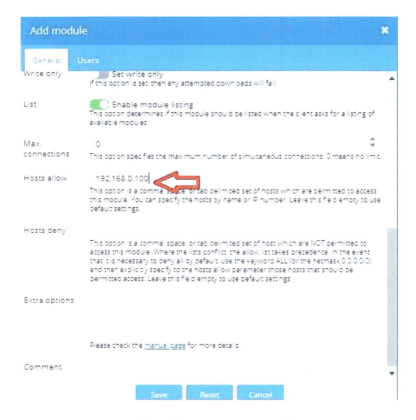

Which hosts are allowed to receive data from.

A user to log on.

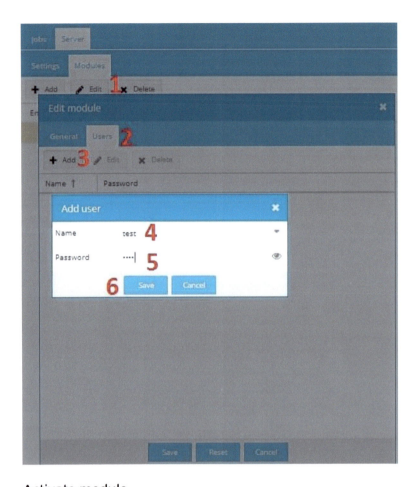

Activate module.

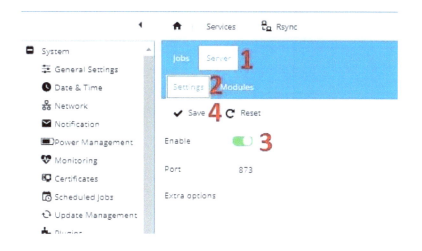

Set up client

Which NAS the data should be copied from.

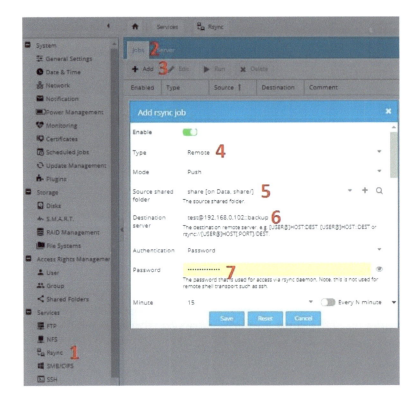

Type: remote

Mode: push

Target server is: test@192.168.0.102 :: backup

Enter the correct path here. Otherwise the connection will not work. And don't forget your password!

The following settings are useful.

The check mark for trial run can also be activated once to see if everything is set up correctly.

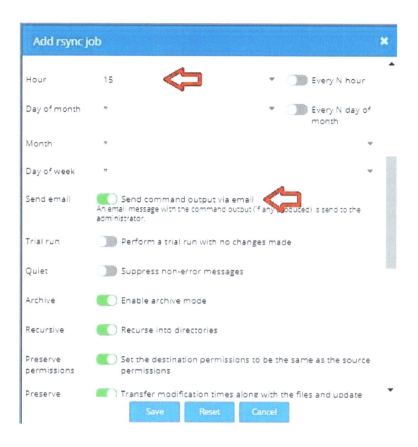

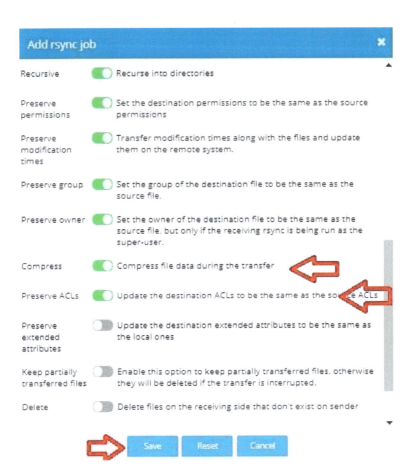

Add rsync job

Recursive	Recurse into directories
Preserve permissions	Set the destination permissions to be the same as the source permissions
Preserve modification times	Transfer modification times along with the files and update them on the remote system.
Preserve group	Set the group of the destination file to be the same as the source file.
Preserve owner	Set the owner of the destination file to be the same as the source file, but only if the receiving rsync is being run as the super-user.
Compress	Compress file data during the transfer
Preserve ACLs	Update the destination ACLs to be the same as the source ACLs
Preserve extended attributes	Update the destination extended attributes to be the same as the local ones
Keep partially transferred files	Enable this option to keep partially transferred files, otherwise they will be deleted if the transfer is interrupted.
Delete	Delete files on the receiving side that don't exist on sender

Save   Reset   Cancel

Recursive means that all data and folders are copied.

Compression saves time during the transfer.

I have not activated deletion. The reason is. If something is accidentally deleted, it will at least not be deleted on the backup page.

It is best to choose the time at night when there is not much going on. And there is no restart either!

ACL and access rights like those from the source. If the hard drive breaks in the original OMV, you can simply reconnect the HDD. Possibly. the main folder still has to be renamed.

If the sending of e-mails is activated, a message should also appear if everything went well.

imprint

© 2019 Randy Bolz

Sterndamm 17

12487 Berlin

Edition (1)

Cover design, illustration: Randy Bolz

Proofreading, proofreading: Randy Bolz

Translation: Randy Bolz

Editor: Randy Bolz

www.ingramcontent.com/pod-product-compliance
Lightning Source LLC
Chambersburg PA
CBHW041155050326
40690CB00004B/570